BOOK 1

Flip & Flop

Written by Jenny Phillips

Illustrated by Denise Hughes

Cover design by Amanda Wood

goodandbeautiful.com

This is Flip.

This is Flop.

Flip is small,
but Flop is not.

In fact, Flop is big.

Flip has spots, but
Flop does not.

Dentist
4pm
PARIS
FLOP

Do you love Flip’s spots?

I do!

Do you like Flop’s snack?

Yuck, I do not!

Flip can do lots of flips.

He can flip by Mom, and he can flip by me.

On the grass he can do six flips.

Can Flop do flips?

No way!

Flop can flop.

Oh, yes, he can flop.

He is a flopping pet.

He flops at this spot, and he flops at that spot.

Look at Flip.

He can dash, and he can zip.

He can jump, and
he can spin.

Flop does not dash or spin.

He . . . flops.

There goes Flip!

He does tricks.

He spins and spins until . . .

Oh no! He crashes, but he will not stop.

He keeps doing tricks.

"Do a trick," I say to Flop.

He just flops.

"Hmmmm . . ." I say. "Flop, you flop a lot."

I say, "Get up, Flop," so he does.

But in a bit, he flops.

I shrug.

"Flop is just a flopping pet."

"Flop is my pal," I say.

I put my hand on him.
"I love this flopping pet."

Flip comes to me, and he gets snug.

"Flip is my pal," I say as I pat him.

"I love this pet that flips and does tricks."

Flip gets snug with Flop.

"They are pals," I say.

Yes, I love Flop.

And I love Flip.

And Flip loves Flop.

And Flop loves Flip.

I tell Mom, "Flip, Flop,
and I are best pals!"

Check out these Level 1A books from

The Good and the Beautiful!

A Dog Named Sniff: Book 1

By Jenny Phillips

Beth's Sheep Ranch: The Yak

By Annabelle Bos

goodandbeautiful.com

Check out these Level 1B books from

The Good and the Beautiful!

Pine Cone Hill: Book 1

By Shannen Yauger

Rolling Thunder: A Hamster's Tale

By Heather Horn

goodandbeautiful.com

1 0NSP460-159744 Printed in USA Jan-2025